MELBOURNE TRAVEL GUIDE 2024:

Discovering Melbourne's beauty and treasures, including top restaurants and accommodations

Havilah F. Mills

Table of Contents

Chapter 1

Introduction to Melbourne

Welcome to Melbourne

Melbourne is a city that deftly combines a rich tapestry of cultural heritage with contemporary refinement. Melbourne, the dynamic capital of the state of Victoria, is tucked away on Australia's southeast coast and entices tourists with a wide range of attractions.

You'll be enthralled by the city's dynamic architecture as you move about it, where modern skyscrapers and old sites coexist. As a center of culture, the famous Federation Square hosts festivals and events that capture the unique character of the city. Discover hidden treasures in the shape of hip bars, quaint cafés, and boutique stores by taking a leisurely walk along the quaint alleyways covered with street art.

Melbourne is well known for its food scene, with a wide variety of top-notch eateries to suit all tastes. The city's culinary options are a tribute to its many cultural influences, whether you're enjoying a delicious breakfast in one of the hip suburbs or tasting international cuisines in the CBD.

Since Melbourne is known for its intense love of sports, sports fans will find themselves in paradise. The Melbourne Cricket Ground (MCG) is a magnificent example of a sports coliseum, drawing crowds of thousands of fans with its Australian Rules football and cricket events. Major athletic events bring the city to life, fostering a spirit of enthusiasm and unity.

The Royal Botanic Gardens is a haven of peace for nature enthusiasts in the middle of the bustle of the city. Those looking for a peaceful escape from the bustle of the city can find solace in the verdant surroundings, colorful flowers, and tranquil lakes. If you're up for an adventure, you may visit the scenic Great Ocean Road, which connects the vast Southern Ocean with striking cliffs and is only a short drive away.

Melbourne's abundance of galleries, theaters, and music venues is proof of its dedication to the arts. The Arts Centre Melbourne presents a diverse range of activities, including classical concerts and avant-garde theatrical shows, while the National Gallery of Victoria displays an extraordinary collection of art that spans centuries.

Melbourne is essentially a city that embraces variety and encourages discovery. Recognized for their warmth and friendliness, its residents add to the welcome vibe that characterizes the city. Whether you're a sports enthusiast, a cultural vulture, or just looking for a great gastronomic experience,

Melbourne welcomes you to immerse yourself in its vibrant tapestry and make memories that will last a long time after your trip. Welcome to Melbourne, a city where life is celebrated and stories can be found around every turn.

An overview of Melbourne

Melbourne, the vibrant, multicultural center of Australia's southeast coast, provides a fascinating fusion of modernism, history, and a unique sense of individuality. This city, which serves as Victoria's capital, is a kaleidoscope of experiences that invites both residents and tourists to discover its many facets.

Melbourne's skyline is a fascinating display of architectural forms coming together at first glance, which is a monument to the city's progress throughout time. The way that modern, sleek buildings are juxtaposed with ancient sites like Flinders Street Station demonstrates the city's dedication to both embracing change and maintaining its legacy. A famous gathering place, Federation Square, is alive with activity, with events that showcase Melbourne's thriving cultural scene.

Art takes center stage in the city's alleyways, where one can feel the pulse of the city. Vibrant street art adorning these little streets reveals a creatively hidden world complete with unique businesses, quaint cafés, and unusual bars. Discovering these alleyways is like traversing a live painting, with every turn revealing a different aspect of Melbourne's creative culture.

Melbourne is known for being a foodie haven, with a diverse range of cuisines to suit every palate. The city is a culinary lover's dream come true, from the flavorful restaurants to the fragrant coffee culture that permeates its streets. There is no shortage of delicious food in the Central Business District, and there are many undiscovered secrets on the outskirts.

Melbourne is a haven for sports fans. During Australian Rules football and cricket matches, the Melbourne Cricket Ground (MCG) is filled with the thunderous applause of fervent supporters. Beyond the stadium, Melbourne's sports culture is evident in the way that big events turn the city into a thriving center of enthusiasm and friendship.

Nature lovers don't have to go far to get comfort. Explore a wide variety of plant life as you meander through lush landscapes at the Royal Botanic Gardens, a tranquil haven in the middle of the metropolis. The Great Ocean Road, which is just a short drive away, offers a stunning view of the Southern Ocean and coastal cliffs, demonstrating Melbourne's closeness to other natural beauties.

Melbourne is clearly committed to the arts, as seen by the rich tapestry of creative expression on display at places like the National Gallery of Victoria. With its characteristic spire, the Arts Centre Melbourne is home to a wide range of events that suit the varied cultural tastes of the city, including avant-garde theatrical shows and classical concerts.

Melbourne is essentially a diverse city that encourages exploration and a sense of community. The hospitable ambiance of the city is enhanced by its inhabitants, who are renowned for their kindness and compassion. Melbourne is more than just a place to visit; it's an experience that takes place amid alleyways brimming with legends, stadiums resounding with applause, and cultural institutions mirroring a city constantly changing in character. This is Melbourne, a city that beckons you to take in the depths of its offers and lose yourself in its vibrant story.

Melbourne's distinct cultural atmosphere

Melbourne's cultural atmosphere is a symphony of innovation and variety, creating a tapestry that captures the essence of the city. Melbourne's multiculturalism is ingrained in the city and is seen in many aspects of everyday life, including the food scene, the arts, and community festivals.

The melting-pot nature of the city is reflected in its cuisine and culture. Discovering the food scene is similar to setting off on a worldwide culinary adventure. Melbourne is a food lover's paradise, from the fragrant laneway coffee culture to the wide variety of ethnic cuisines tucked away in its suburbs. The city's image as a global melting pot of cuisines stems from every restaurant, café, and market stall that exists there.

Melbourne is unique in that it has a constant dedication to the arts. The city is a creative hub, as seen by its theaters, galleries, and street art. As you meander through the winding lanes, you'll come upon a live canvas that has been adorned by both local and foreign artists. With its vast collection of works from all eras, the National Gallery of Victoria acts as a cultural focal point, while smaller galleries dotted across the city display up-and-coming artists.

Melbourne's live music venues and theaters are testaments to the city's passion for the performing arts. For orchestra concerts, ballets, and plays, the Arts Centre Melbourne is a shining star. In the meantime, the city's small-scale live music culture is thriving and provides a stage for both domestic and foreign performers to display their skills in settings ranging from modern clubs to medieval taverns.

Melbourne supports a grassroots cultural movement in addition to the established arts. The calendar is filled with festivals and community gatherings that honor everything from modern inventions to cultural legacies. Moomba Festival, White Night Melbourne, and the Melbourne International Film Festival are just a few examples of the many cultural events that the city has to offer and invite locals and tourists to partake in.

The open cultural pulse of Melbourne encourages everyone to take part in the vibrant creative scene of the city. People themselves add to this rich cultural fabric with a variety of origins and viewpoints. Melbourne's cultural mood is a constantly changing representation of the city's soul, whether you're enjoying international cuisines, touring cutting-edge art installations, or losing yourself in the exuberant atmosphere of a festival. It's a location where innovation and tradition collide, and diversity is welcomed and honored—a representation of the lively spirit that characterizes this treasure of Australian culture.

Chapter 2

Means of Getting to Melbourne

How to fly to Melbourne

Traveling by plane to Melbourne is a thrilling experience that combines the thrill of adventure with the convenience of air travel. Usually, the trip starts with the laborious process of selecting a flight, which involves comparing many airlines, departure times, and ticket categories. The countdown to departure starts as soon as the flight is chosen, which could cause some excitement as well as anxiety before a trip.

There is a flurry of activity on the day of departure as everyone packs, verifies paperwork, and makes sure that every necessary item fits into the luggage. Whether it's a fast cab trip or a leisurely drive, getting to the airport contributes to the feeling of embarkation. Both seasoned travelers and those venturing into the world of air travel for the first time are drawn to the vitality of the airport itself, a hive of human activity.

It may be quite overwhelming to go through security checks, the maze-like duty-free stores, and the check-in procedure. Still, they are necessary stages on the way to the exit. Excitement is increased as one watches aircraft taxiing on the tarmac, preparing to spread their wings and take off. When you board the plane, the voyage officially begins as you leave the ground and enter the air.

The sound of the engines fades into the background after you're comfortable in your seat. Every little thing, from the menu options to the safety demonstration by the cabin staff, adds to the special ambience of flying. Throughout the journey, the view outside the window—whether it is a wide expanse of water, a cityscape, or a cloudscape—becomes a captivating companion.

The hours spent in the air may be used for introspection, reading, or catching up on the newest in-flight entertainment for those who value the trip as much as the destination. The view below changes as the plane gets closer to Melbourne, showing a mix of open spaces, urban development, and the unique Australian topography.

The aerial portion of the journey comes to an end with the descent into Melbourne. With a mix of relief and excitement, the landing signals the start of discovery in a city renowned for its rich cultural heritage, array of attractions, and friendly people. Flying becomes more than simply a mode of transportation; it becomes an essential component of the whole travel experience, combining the distinct appeal of the voyage with the thrill of arriving.

Options for Transportation in Melbourne

There is a symphony of transit alternatives available for navigating Melbourne's colorful streets, each adding a note to the city's dynamic beat. There are many options available to you as you navigate this urban terrain, making your trip as varied as the city itself.

With an almost choreographed elegance, Melbourne's famed trams, a vital component of the city's public transportation system, wind through the streets. Their distinctive rattle, which reverberates across the city, is a well-known sound. Getting on a tram is more than just a way to go about; it's a way to see Melbourne life as it comes in all its fluctuations. You may take a leisurely tour of the main sights on the nostalgic and free City Circle Tram, which lets you experience the spirit of the city at your own speed.

Melbourne's vast network of bike lanes embraces the culture of riding two wheels and encourages you to ride your way across the city's mosaic of neighborhoods. Dedicated bicycle routes and bike-sharing programs appeal to both enthusiastic riders and relaxed tourists, offering a different viewpoint on the city's parks and buildings.

Taxis and ridesharing services are widely available in Melbourne, providing a door-to-door experience for those who want the convenience of four wheels. The city's signature yellow taxis are an integral part of the landscape, and the ridesharing movement has given this time-honored form of transportation a contemporary update.

The rail system, which runs like veins across the city, offers a quick way to go from one part of Melbourne to another. The train ride becomes a miniature representation of the city's diversity, reflecting the variety of cultures and lifestyles that characterize Melbourne, from the busy Southern Cross Station to the suburban stations.

Automobile lovers may enjoy the independence of driving and take their time seeing the city and its environs. Melbourne's well-kept road system links the city to its suburbs, where beautiful drives and undiscovered treasures are waiting to be discovered.

There are more than just traditional modes of transportation in Melbourne. River boats meander across the Yarra, providing a peaceful diversion from the hustle and bustle of the city. Traveling by boat offers a distinctive view of the city's skyline and a new angle on well-known sites.

Traveling becomes a multidimensional experience in Melbourne thanks to the integrated network of transportation alternatives. Every form of transportation adds something different to Melbourne's transportation environment, whether you like the luxury of a vehicle, the flexibility of a bicycle, the speedy efficiency of a train, or the historic elegance of a tram. Each method of transportation adds a chapter to the story of discovering this fascinating city, so it's not just about going from point A to point B—it's about fully immersing oneself in the experience.

Airports in Melbourne

Tullamarine Airport, Melbourne's air transport hub, is a busy hub that links the city to locations throughout the globe. Its immense space, teeming with activity, serves as the beginning point of an endless number of excursions, each with a unique story and end point.

You can feel the airport's vibrancy as soon as you enter the terminal. With a swarm of activity, the check-in counters watch the planned mayhem of tourists setting off on adventures. The sound of rolling baggage on shiny floors and far-off remarks over the intercom combine to produce a symphony that evokes the excitement of leaving.

Passport controls, an obligatory formality, bring you into the departure lounge, an area where time stands still. Duty-free stores entice shoppers with a diverse selection of things, ranging from upscale merchandise to traditional Australian keepsakes. For those looking for a brief moment of relaxation, cafés and lounges provide a safe refuge where visitors may have a last taste of the local food or a cup of coffee before boarding.

The international terminal of Melbourne Airport reflects the multicultural nature of the city. The realm of convergent cultures is accessed via passport control. Duty-free shopping becomes an international exhibition with merchandise from all around the world. As you get closer to the departure gate, the excitement increases since each flight board shows a matrix of destinations, each with its own unique appeal.

As you board the plane, you can see the baggage handlers and ground personnel doing a dance to prepare for departure. The aerial chapter begins with the sound of the engines, and the urban gives way to a patchwork of landscapes, seas, and far-off vistas. Whether it's a little hop or cross-continental travel, the aircraft itself becomes a paused point in time, a transitional area between departure and arrival.

When you return, Melbourne Airport seems like a warm hug that greets both locals and tourists. The sounds of happy hugs and tales exchanged reverberate from the arrival gate, a scene of reunions and pleasantries. Every suitcase on the luggage carousel becomes a container for memories and mementos, transforming it into a little version of the globe.

Melbourne's aviation history is enhanced by the unique appeal of Avalon Airport, which lies beyond Tullamarine. It is a different kind of gateway that accommodates both local and international aircraft and has a more relaxed atmosphere. Its efficient facilities and close proximity to the city set it apart in Melbourne's aviation scene.

Each thread in the tapestry of Tullamarine and Avalon, Melbourne's airports, tells a tale of discovery, connection, and the easy movement of people and experiences. Melbourne's airports are a major part of the stories of those who travel through its gates, from the exhilaration of takeoff to the welcome of arrival. Each voyage becomes a new chapter in the city's dynamic story.

Melbourne's Public Transportation

Melbourne's public transport system is a vibrant network that connects many districts and creates a rich tapestry of passenger experiences. The famous trams, whose rhythmic clatter reverberates through the streets and provides a unique soundtrack to urban life, are at the center of this complex network.

The tram system in Melbourne is more than just a means of transportation; it represents the spirit of the city. With its charming historical design, the City Circle Tram encircles the central business area and offers a free, leisurely trip past some of the most famous sites in the city to both residents and tourists. Taking a tram ride transforms into a voyage across space and time that offers views of both contemporary urban life and ancient buildings.

The railroads that wind through the city and its suburbs are a nice addition to the trams. Melbourne's rail network serves as the city's main thoroughfare, effectively moving passengers to their destinations from the bustling platforms of Flinders Street Station to the more sedate outlying stations. The sound of trains in motion and the repetitive banging of shutting doors combine to create a symphony that emphasizes the everyday commute.

The adaptable workhorses of public transportation, buses maneuver through Melbourne's streets, making their way to nooks and crannies that trams and trains are unable to access. Bus stations, sometimes embellished with vibrant street art, function as gathering places for those starting short and long travels. Through the passing landscape, the bus trip becomes a window into the areas it passes through, providing a peek at local life.

The key to this public transport mosaic is the myki card, which is a commonplace item in Melbourne commuters' pockets. It becomes second nature to swipe on and off, a ritual that allows one to access the city's movement. Myki Card is the conductor that conducts passengers through the urban symphony, whether it is the daily grind of the nine-to-five or a leisurely discovery of Melbourne's hidden jewels.

Melbourne's dedication to environmentally friendly transportation is shown by the city's network of bike lanes, which encourage riders to cycle through the streets. Dedicated bike lanes and programs foster a two-wheeled harmony that blends in with the urban environment while offering an environmentally beneficial option for people looking to travel more actively.

A beautiful and peaceful diversion from the bustle of the city may be found via ferry services along the Yarra River. Offering a distinctive viewpoint of Melbourne's skyline, the soft sound of the water lapping against the ferry's hull acts as a counterbalance to the bustle of the city.

In Melbourne, using public transit is more than simply a way to go from place A to place B—it's an engaging journey that allows you to discover the beating core of the city. Every kind of transportation adds to the complex story of urban mobility, whether it is the eco-consciousness of cycling, the efficiency of trains, the historic appeal of trams, or the adaptability of buses. Melbourne's public transport system connects people and places in a symphony of movement and life, serving as more than simply a mode of transportation—it's an essential component of the city's identity.

Chapter 3

Accommodation options in Melbourne

Melbourne's Best Hotels

Of course! Melbourne's hospitality sector is lively and diversified, with several excellent hotels that suit different budgets and interests. Located along the famous Southbank promenade, The Langham is well-known for its luxurious decor and first-rate service. Offering visitors an opulent experience, this five-star hotel provides stunning views of the Melbourne cityscape and Yarra River.

An iconic hotel that offers a unique combination of contemporary amenities and historical charm is The Hotel Windsor. Founded in 1883, it radiates sophistication from bygone eras while deftly blending modern conveniences. This hotel, which is close to Parliament House, is a classic option for anybody who likes a hint of Victorian splendor.

If you're more into modern architecture and creative flare, the Adelphi Hotel on Flinders Lane is a work of art in and of itself. This hotel offers visitors who value innovation in every aspect an engaging experience with its distinctive design features and boutique sensibility.

Conversely, QT Melbourne provides a contemporary and lively atmosphere while being tucked away in the Central Business District. This hotel caters to the discriminating guest looking for a chic and lively setting with an emphasis on contemporary aesthetics and a whimsical touch.

Just outside of Melbourne, The Mansion Hotel & Spa at Werribee Park is a hidden treasure for anybody looking for a getaway among beautiful vegetation. Enclosed by vast grounds and housed in a historic home, it provides a peaceful haven that is easily accessible to the city.

In summary, Melbourne's best hotels provide accommodations that suit a wide range of tastes, so each guest can choose a place to stay that suits their needs, whether it is traditional luxury, cutting-edge design, or a tasteful combination of both.

Melbourne Boutique Hotels

Discovering Melbourne's boutique hotels offers a wealth of unusual lodging options that each provide a unique fusion of personality, flair, and attentive service. The Cullen, one of the Art Series hotels situated in the hip Prahran district, is a noteworthy choice. With rooms featuring unique artwork by well-known Australian artist Adam Cullen, it combines hospitality and art flawlessly, giving visitors an utterly immersive experience.

The Gertrude Street Residence, located in the center of Fitzroy, perfectly embodies Melbourne's free-spirited vibe. With a carefully chosen assortment of self-contained flats, this boutique jewel lets visitors fully experience the unique charm of one of Melbourne's trendiest districts.

The Lyall Hotel in South Yarra is a notable choice for anyone seeking a little of the past paired with modern sophistication. This elegant boutique hotel, with all suites, offers well-appointed, roomy rooms. Its attentive attention to detail and customized treatment give visitors the impression that they are living in an opulent home away from home.

Located in the lively St. Kilda district, The Prince Hotel is a boutique accommodation that skillfully combines contemporary style with a dash of beachside charm. With a view of Port Phillip Bay, it offers a chic but relaxed setting and many dining choices, including the well-known Prince Dining Room.

In the meantime, the Royal Botanic Gardens' neighbor, United Places Botanic Gardens, raises the bar for boutique luxury. It provides a small and unique refuge with only twelve rooms that are all beautifully furnished, giving visitors a feeling of privacy in the middle of the city.

These Melbourne boutique accommodations provide guests with more than simply lodging; they also provide a carefully chosen experience that captures the vibrant and varied character of the city, making every visit unforgettable and distinctively Melbourne.

Melbourne's Affordable Choices

Finding reasonably priced lodging in Melbourne provides access to a range of choices that let visitors enjoy the city without going over budget. Located in the center of Melbourne, the Melbourne Central YHA offers budget-friendly lodging without sacrificing location. Being close to popular destinations like Federation Square and Queen Victoria Market makes it a great option for budget-conscious travelers who want to see Melbourne's most famous sites without breaking the bank.

Nestled in the vibrant St Kilda neighborhood, Habitat HQ is an affordable hostel with a laid-back, beachy ambiance. Because of its social areas, it's a terrific option for single visitors or those looking for a more engaging stay. For visitors on a tight budget, the adjacent St. Kilda Beach and Luna Park provide even another level of enjoyment.

Fitzroy's The Nunnery is a great place to find a unique combination of quirky and affordable. Located in a remodeled 19th-century convent, it provides inexpensive, charming dormitory-style lodging. For tourists on a tight budget seeking a genuine Melbourne experience, the Fitzroy neighborhood, renowned for its street art and hip eateries, adds to the attraction.

Discovering Footscray presents the Footscray Motor Inn, another affordable treasure. Though it's a little farther out from the CBD, this choice offers cozy lodging at a lower cost. For tourists on a tight budget, Footscray's colorful and ethnic atmosphere—combined with a varied food scene—adds another level of discovery.

Budget travel around Melbourne is now considerably easier, thanks to the tram system. Located next to the Queen Victoria Market, the Melbourne Metro YHA provides a handy and reasonably priced starting point for visitors using public transit to go about the city. For those on a tight budget, the hostel's community kitchen offers affordable food alternatives.

These inexpensive things to do in Melbourne show that visiting the city doesn't have to be expensive. Hostels in convenient locations and distinctive lodgings in hip areas are just two of the many options available to budget-conscious travelers who still want to experience Melbourne's spirit.

Chapter 4

Exploring Melbourne City Districts

The Central Business District (CBD) of Melbourne

Australia's second-largest city, Melbourne, is characterized by a lively and busy Central Business District (CBD) that embodies the city's dynamism. Located in the core of Melbourne, the CBD is the hub of the city's culture, business, and daily activities. The CBD presents a visually stunning contrast of old and new, appealing to both locals and tourists with its unique blend of contemporary buildings and antique architecture.

Tall and a monument to the city's architectural brilliance, the Eureka Tower and other renowned buildings dominate the skyline of the Melbourne CBD. This massive structure serves as a reminder of the city's vastness by providing panoramic views of the spreading metropolis below, in addition to adding to the metropolitan silhouette.

Melbourne's central business district is a sensory journey through the streets. The city has a well-known coffee culture that has grown to be an essential part of its character, and the scent of freshly brewed coffee fills the air. The streets are lined with restaurants and sidewalk cafés that invite customers to enjoy cuisine from all around the world.

A historical site and architectural marvel, Flinders Street Station connects several rail lines and acts as a gathering place for both residents and visitors. A lasting representation of Melbourne's rich history and cultural importance is the station's striking yellow facade.

The Melbourne CBD is a canvas for public art, with colorful street art lining laneways and alleys behind its business façade. The city's standing as a refuge for cultural and artistic undertakings is enhanced by these creative manifestations. Melbourne has more to offer than just its business façade when you take the time to explore these hidden jewels.

The Yarra River brings a touch of nature to the cityscape as it meanders softly through the CBD. Parks and promenades along the river provide a peaceful haven where locals and tourists may relax in the middle of the bustle of the city. The contrast between buildings and water makes for a beautiful scene, particularly at night when the city lights reflect off the surface of the river.

When it comes to retail therapy, the Melbourne CBD is an absolute haven for shoppers. Those who like luxury and fashion are drawn to Bourke Street Mall because of its flagship stores and boutiques. The maze-like alleys are home to a variety of individual businesses that provide distinctive merchandise and enhance Melbourne's standing as a fashion-forward city.

The Melbourne CBD is alive with cultural events and entertainment, in addition to business and commerce. Federation Square and the Arts Centre Melbourne are major cultural centers that hold a wide range of events all year long, including festivals, exhibits, and performances. These spaces encourage creativity and a sense of community, which helps Melbourne maintain its reputation as a major cultural hub for the world.

To sum up, the Melbourne Central Business District encompasses more than just a collection of skyscrapers and business buildings. It's a living, breathing thing that captures the spirit of Melbourne and its people, history, innovation, and culture all blended together in a beautiful whole.

Fitzroy: Melbourne's Arts & Culture District

Fitzroy is a dynamic tapestry of arts and culture that combines a modern creative attitude with a deep heritage. Fitzroy, a vibrant center that supports creative expression in all of its forms, is tucked away just north of the Melbourne CBD.

Fitzroy's diverse street art culture is one of its most distinctive aspects. Building facades are decorated with a kaleidoscope of colors and forms as you meander through their laneways and lanes. Fitzroy is transformed into an outdoor gallery by these murals, which often change with the seasons and highlight the neighborhood's dedication to encouraging creativity in unexpected places.

The center of Fitzroy's creative community, Gertrude Street, is a microcosm of artistic variety. Independent studios and galleries in this area display a wide range of modern art pieces. Fitzroy's dedication to pushing the frontiers of art is embodied in Gertrude Street, which features both provocative exhibits and avant-garde works.

Fitzroy is a live music lover's paradise, even outside of the visual arts. Famous suburbia locations like The Workers Club and the Evelyn Hotel are alive with the sounds of both well-known performers and up-and-coming local bands. The sound of indie, rock, and techno rhythms permeates the air, creating a culture where people gather and music flourishes.

Fitzroy's dedication to fostering creativity is seen in its communal areas. With its ancient design, Fitzroy Town Hall functions as a venue for cultural events and gatherings in addition to being the city's administrative hub. Parks in the area, such as Edinburgh Gardens, provide a verdant haven for open-air events, festivals, and group get-togethers.

On occasions like the Gertrude Street Projection Festival, when the neighborhood is transformed into a stunning exhibition of light and multimedia art, Fitzroy's sense of community is evident. Fitzroy is known for being a creative melting pot, and this yearly festival highlights the joint efforts of both local and foreign artists.

Many of the cafés and restaurants in Fitzroy also function as galleries, adding to the area's creative vibe. Drinking coffee becomes a multimodal experience as customers discover locally sourced tastes and are surrounded by art that has been carefully chosen. Fitzroy's varied and dynamic food culture is a reflection of the neighborhood's dedication to creativity and individual expression.

Fitzroy has shown its commitment to diversity by endorsing community-driven projects. Co-working spaces, cultural groups, and artist-run spaces work together to create an atmosphere that is unrestricted by creativity. Fitzroy's markets, where regional craftsmen display their wares, foster a sense of community by providing a forum for discussion between the makers and the consumers.

Fitzroy is really more than just a neighborhood; it's a living example of how innovation and tradition, history and modern expression, can coexist. Its walls record the tales of a society that lives off creative inquiry, and its streets resound with the footsteps of those who have come before. Fitzroy is more than just a place to visit; it's a place where the past and the future continue to interact, demonstrating Melbourne's unwavering dedication to the arts.

St. Kilda: Seaside and Nightlife

Melbourne's famous St Kilda area beckons with sun, beaches, and a bustling nightlife scene. Tucked away on the banks of Port Phillip Bay, St. Kilda is home to a beach that has come to represent leisure and well-being. But beyond the sun-kissed dunes is a multidimensional community that skillfully combines beachside beauty with a wide range of leisure opportunities.

With its tempting waves and golden expanse, St. Kilda Beach never fails to draw in both residents and visitors. The beach provides a haven for anyone looking to escape the bustle of the city, whether they want to take a leisurely walk down the palm-lined promenade or cool off in the water. Stretching out into the shimmering seas, the famed St. Kilda Pier is not only a beautiful viewpoint but also evidence of the suburb's historical importance.

The lively heartbeat of St. Kilda's nightlife district comes alive as the sun sets over the water. With its distinctive bakery shops and unique stores, Acland Street transforms into a bustling promenade that brings together live music and delicious food. St. Kilda's eating scene, which offers a global gastronomic adventure, reflects the suburb's multicultural ethos and ranges from hip cafés to elegant restaurants.

Luna Park is a permanent representation of St. Kilda's carefree nature, rising tall at the start of Acland Street. Luna Park has been enthralling tourists with its famous entrance—a massive smiling face—since the early 20th century. Families and thrill-seekers alike find the amusement park to be a timeless attraction because of its vintage rides and carnival ambiance.

The esplanade at St. Kilda serves as a venue for festivals and cultural events in addition to providing a lovely setting for beachgoers. Every year, the St. Kilda Festival, a celebration of music, the arts, and community, turns the shoreline into a colorful canvas filled with artistic interpretations and performances. This celebration perfectly captures St. Kilda's mission to promote a feeling of belonging and pleasure among everyone.

The Palais Theatre, a magnificent architectural treasure on the St. Kilda skyline, is a must-see for anybody looking for a dose of cultural adventure. The Palais Theatre brings sophistication to St. Kilda's entertainment offerings with its varied program of concerts and dramatic shows. Its lavish design and beachfront surroundings make going to a performance here a really immersive experience.

St. Kilda's reputation as Melbourne's entertainment center is further cemented by its unique mix of pubs and live music venues. The area offers a variety of venues to suit different interests and moods, from boisterous pubs with live local bands to cozy jazz clubs. The Espy, often called The Esplanade Hotel, is a cultural landmark that has fostered Australian musicians for many years, demonstrating St. Kilda's ongoing impact on the industry.

To sum up, St. Kilda offers a seductive mix of vibrant entertainment and sun-kissed relaxation. Its esplanade, beach, and cultural hubs weave a harmonious picture that beckons discovery and joy. St. Kilda is more than simply a place to visit; it's a way of life, a sensory encounter that embodies Melbourne's bohemian charm and creative energy.

Chapter 5

Art and Culture in Melbourne

Street Art on Melbourne's Hosier Lane

A live example of Melbourne's dynamic street art scene, Hosier Lane is a hidden gem in the center of the city's commercial sector. What was once a quiet little alleyway has been converted into a vibrant outdoor gallery that features a constantly changing mosaic of innovation, expression, and color.

Strolling around Hosier Lane is like entering another realm where traditional artistic limitations vanish and are replaced by an unbridled burst of creativity. Murals, stencils, and graffiti cover every square inch of the laneway, each adding to the story of Melbourne's street art movement and conveying a different tale.

The fleeting quality of the place, along with the completed artworks, is what makes Hosier Lane so beautiful. Global artists gather here to make their impression, resulting in a vibrant and ever-evolving landscape. It is evidence of the transience of street art, since one day's masterwork may be replaced by another's artwork the next day.

It's amazing how many different themes and styles there are. A harmonic cacophony of abstract artwork, wacky characters, social satire, and political messages coexist. The walls of this little alleyway are home to a worldwide conversation between local and international artists.

The interactive quality of Hosier Lane's artwork is what really sets it apart. In this outdoor gallery, visitors have an active role as participants rather than spectators. Both visitors and residents interact with the artwork by snapping pictures, setting up postures, and making their own transient imprints. The laneway becomes more dynamic as a result of the ongoing interaction between the art and the viewers, giving it a live, breathing quality.

Hosier Lane exudes a spirit of liberation and defiance that goes beyond its visual appeal. By its very nature, street art disrupts the conventional boundaries of galleries and museums, putting art outside and into the hands of everyone. The laneway is a symbol of Melbourne's innovative and creative culture, which celebrates and accepts the unusual.

But there are some controversial aspects to traveling along Hosier Lane. Because street art is temporary, some pieces may eventually disappear due to weather, redevelopment, or time. Debates about the significance of impermanence in the art world are sparked by the conflict between the ephemeral nature of the medium and the need for preservation.

Hosier Lane is essentially a living, breathing monument to Melbourne's status as a center of culture, rather than just a laneway. It captures the spirit of the city's acceptance of the nonconformist, encouragement of artistic expression, and open invitation to everybody to participate in the dynamic work of art that is Melbourne's street art culture.

Chapter 6

Culinary Delights in Melbourne

Melbourne's top restaurants

Melbourne is home to some of the best restaurants in the city, offering a fascinating trip via inventive cuisine and a varied range of sensations. Tucked away in Ripponlea, Attica is a culinary treasure that is well-known not only in Melbourne but across the world. Attica, which is well-known for Chef Ben Shewry's creative approach, is a multi-sensory experience that combines indigenous Australian foods with cutting-edge methods.

With its move into the city center, Vue de Monde actually raises the bar for dining experiences. Situated at the summit of the Rialto building, this restaurant offers expansive vistas over Melbourne in addition to Chef Shannon Bennett's painstakingly prepared meals, which embody a contemporary take on traditional French cuisine.

Nobu Melbourne at the Crown complex offers a unique dining experience for customers looking for a blend of Peruvian and Japanese elements. Chef Nobu Matsuhisa's distinctive dishes showcase the exquisite blending of tastes, creating a gastronomic journey that surpasses conventional limitations.

Located in the heart of Flinders Lane, Cumulus Inc. offers a modern take on Melbourne's café culture. Under the direction of Chef Andrew McConnell, the cuisine features foods that are in-season and locally produced, and its light-filled, stylish atmosphere makes it a perennial favorite for both residents and tourists.

Under the direction of Chef Neil Perry, the Rockpool Bar & Grill in the Southbank district is a shrine to the ideal steak. For those who love meat, the restaurant's dedication to serving only the best pieces of meat, perfectly grilled and paired with an extensive wine selection, guarantees a decadent experience.

Chin Chin, on Flinders Lane, is another place to highlight Melbourne's variety. This vibrant restaurant with a Thai influence, renowned for its flavorful food and energetic ambiance, is a monument to the city's diverse culinary scene. Chef Benjamin Cooper has created a menu with a variety of sharing dishes that entice the palate.

These are just a few samples of Melbourne's diverse culinary scene, where each eatery tells a different tale with its own blend of ingredients, atmosphere, and cooking techniques. Melbourne's greatest restaurants provide a culinary trip that highlights the city's vibrant and ever-evolving food culture, ranging from fine dining venues to offbeat eateries.

Melbourne Laneway Cafés

Nestled in the obscure corners that characterize the city's urban environment, Melbourne's alley cafés are the throbbing core of the city's coffee culture. Wander down these alleyways, and you'll find a plethora of distinctive, character-filled cafés that capture the bohemian vibe of the city while serving excellent coffee.

Melbourne's café culture is revitalized by the alleyway known as Degraves Street, which is always a favorite. There are little cafés all over the cobblestone sidewalk, each with its own flair. Degraves Street provides a sensory experience that blends the rich scent of freshly brewed coffee with the varied rush of city life. It has everything from hidden jewels to intimate locations with outdoor seats.

Another famous alley, Hardware Lane, is a busy cluster of cafés that eloquently combine old-world charm with modern sensibilities. The cafés here open out into the cobblestone path, providing an al fresco dining experience against the background of old buildings. It's the ideal place to have a coffee and take in the colorful street art that covers the walls.

It's like entering a coffee-fueled paradise as you explore Center Place. This little alleyway is decorated with vibrant umbrellas that are strung above, producing a rainbow of colors. The cafés here have a cozy, homey vibe that entices both residents and tourists to enter a world where the creative energy of the surrounding walls covered with graffiti blends harmoniously with the perfume of freshly ground coffee.

Nestled along Union Lane are a series of undiscovered treasures where artisan coffee and eccentric décor rule supreme. The smart residents visit these alley cafés because they provide a break from the busy downtown streets. Because of the small-scale settings and the resulting feeling of community, Union Lane is a haven for anyone looking for some peace and quiet in the middle of the bustling city.

Melbourne's laneway cafés are vibrant centers that perfectly capture the essence of the city—much more than simply somewhere to get a cup of coffee. With every drink offering a glimpse into Melbourne's dynamic and ever-changing culture, every laneway café adds to the city's status as the world's coffee capital, from the olfactory appeal of freshly roasted beans to the camaraderie of conversations exchanged.

Melbourne's Queen Victoria Market

A dynamic tapestry of sights, sounds, and smells, Queen Victoria Market is popularly known by locals as "Vic Market" and is a vital part of Melbourne's cultural scene. This ancient market, which spans a large area in the center of the city, was founded in the 19th century and has since grown to become a thriving center of community and trade.

It's like walking into a sensory nirvana when you enter the market. A symphony of market cries complements the vibrant ambiance, with merchants fervently promoting their fresh produce, handcrafted wares, and delicious delicacies. It's more than simply a market; it's an immersive experience where you can feel the pulse of Melbourne's varied food scene all around you.

The market's rainbow of fresh food is one of its distinguishing qualities. The booths are stacked high with seasonal treats from nearby farms, and the colorful assortment of fruits, vegetables, and herbs makes for a visual feast. Every trip to the market is an occasion to celebrate the abundant agricultural produce of the area, from the vibrant hues of heritage tomatoes to the aromatic herbs that invite culinary experimentation.

You will come across the Meat Hall, a sanctuary for foodies and a tribute to carnivores, as you wind through the maze-like passageways. The butchers' booths highlight premium cuts, meats that are ethically sourced, and a degree of skill that highlights Melbourne's dedication to fine dining. The smell of roasting meats and grilled sausages contributes to the carnivalesque ambience.

Gourmet pleasure aficionados will find a veritable gold mine in the Deli Hall. A well-chosen assortment of cheeses, olives, antipasti, and other culinary treats are available here. The enthusiastic vendors are eager to share their expertise and provide samples, turning the purchasing experience into a multisensory investigation of tastes and sensations.

Beyond the delicious food, Queen Victoria Market is a treasure trove for those looking for one-of-a-kind goods and handmade items. Melbourne's creative and diverse attitude is reflected in the general merchandise sector, which is a veritable treasure trove of unique things, including handcrafted jewelry, vintage apparel, and a variety of eccentric products. It's like going on a treasure hunt as you explore these booths; every find reveals a tale of artistry and skill.

The market is a cultural melting pot in addition to a place to buy and eat. The International Food Court, where a wide variety of cuisines live peacefully, is a reflection of its diversity. Melbourne's gastronomic variety, which ranges from Turkish kebabs to Spanish paella, is reflected in its ranking as one of the most multicultural cities in the world.

Queen Victoria Market is more than simply a market place; it's a dynamic representation of Melbourne's past, present, and future. Locals congregate there, visitors immerse themselves in the beating heart of the city, and the spirit of Melbourne permeates every booth, dish, and conversation. Not only is it a market, but it's also a symbol of culture—one that keeps changing but never wavers from the customs that have made it a cherished part of Melbourne culture.

Unique dining experiences in Melbourne

Melbourne's eating scene is above and beyond the norm, providing a mosaic of distinctive culinary experiences that combine originality, innovation, and a hint of avant-garde flare. The city is a foodie's paradise, offering everything from underground supper clubs to immersive culinary adventures for those looking for more than simply a meal—a trip into the unusual.

Melbourne is home to a unique phenomenon in the form of hidden pubs and secret dinner clubs. Hiding behind modest façades, these secretive enterprises invite the knowledgeable to go into a realm of concealed extravagance. Savoring finely prepared beverages and unique cuisine in private, speakeasy-inspired settings is made even more enjoyable by the excitement of discovery. It combines the thrill of discovering Melbourne's best-kept secrets with gastronomic brilliance.

The city is home to cutting-edge restaurants that blur the boundaries between food and art for people who are looking for a fully immersive eating experience. Come experience Heston Blumenthal's Dinner, which reinvents classic British cuisine with a modern touch. Beyond the plate, food is presented as delicious stories that entice guests to go on a culinary voyage throughout time, demonstrating culinary sorcery.

The Colonial Tramcar Restaurant is raising the bar for dining—literally. Diners enjoy a delicious supper while seeing Melbourne's streets aboard a painstakingly rebuilt tram. Gourmet food, a touch of nostalgia, and the rhythmic hum of the tram combine to offer an exceptional dining experience that combines gastronomic pleasures with a hint of nostalgia.

For those who like unusual experiences, the Croft Institute provides a unique eating experience. With its unique décor and food that defies convention, this former research lab turned restaurant has a quirky appeal of its own. This is an area where experimenting with food goes beyond the confines of the laboratory.

Melbourne's distinctive eating experiences are reflected in its laneway culture, where cafés called Hole in the Wall provide more than simply great coffee. Nestled in small lanes, these hidden jewels astonish and thrill with their unique menus, fostering an intimate ambiance that goes beyond the standard café experience.

Smith & Daughters is a vegan restaurant that defies stereotypes about plant-based food, exemplifying the city's dedication to sustainability and ethical eating. The cuisine highlights Melbourne's proactive commitment to culinary variety and sustainability with its vibrant tastes and creative combinations.

Melbourne offers distinctive eating experiences outside of conventional spaces. Dining experiences are elevated to new heights by rooftop bars and restaurants like Naked in the Sky, both literally and metaphorically. Guests may enjoy creative drinks and a variety of cuisine against the background of the city skyline, combining gourmet enjoyment with panoramic views to create a sensory experience.

Melbourne's culinary story is dynamic and always changing, and every meal is a chance to participate in it. Dining is an art form. Melbourne's distinctive eating experiences, which range from hidden treasures to avant-garde masterpieces, offer not just nourishment but also an exploration of tastes, atmospheres, and tales that showcase the city's limitless imagination and gourmet brilliance.

Chapter 7

Shopping Spots in Melbourne

Melbourne's Bourke Street Mall

Melbourne, Australia's Bourke Street Mall, is a bustling center where the daily commotion of the city reflects its pulse. There's no denying the excitement of this famous pedestrian promenade, where a varied mix of people weave through the maze-like array of boutiques and stores.

A symphony of laughter and conversation blends with the rhythmic buzz of footfall on the pavement as visitors and residents alike move through the mall, each with a distinct objective in mind. Shops with eye-catching displays invite people to stop and look at the newest styles or indulge in some shopping therapy.

In stark contrast to the surrounding contemporary structures, Melbourne Central's Shot Tower remains towering as a mute reminder of the city's industrial past. With their seductive fragrances wafting through the air, cafés and restaurants that spill onto the sidewalk entice those in need of a quick snack or a fix for coffee.

Melbourne's cultural mix is encapsulated in the Bourke Street Mall, which is more than simply a place to shop. Street artists provide a whimsical element to the setting while enthralling spectators with their skills in dance, music, or acrobatics. The shopping center transforms into a stage, and the patrons unintentionally participate in the constantly evolving spectacle taking place in front of them.

Tram tracks set into the pavement reverberate with the sound of passing trams, a tribute to the effective public transport network in the city. The ease with which commuters maneuver through the crowd is evidence of Melbourne's established rhythm, which harmoniously combines work and play.

The city lights come on as the day turns into the evening, illuminating Bourke Street Mall with a cozy glow. With the stores lit up and live music filling the air from surrounding establishments, the setting takes on a whole new charm. The mall becomes a center of nightlife when night falls, a place where the pulse of the city beats at a different pace.

With its blend of business, culture, and community, Bourke Street Mall captures the spirit of Melbourne, a city that feeds off variety, innovation, and the ever-changing tides of urban life. It is a live, breathing example of the vibrancy that characterizes this Australian city, rather than just a commercial district.

Melbourne Chapel Street

Melbourne's Chapel Street is a fascinating avenue that winds through a variety of communities, with each block presenting a distinctive fusion of business, culture, and character. As soon as you walk along this famous street, you're engulfed in a diverse range of experiences that capture the energy and vitality of the city.

South Yarra's Chapel Street stretches out like a treasure trove of upscale boutiques, luxury shops, and sophisticated cafés. Stylists stroll around the chic stores, attracting individuals with an eye for style with their window displays showcasing the newest trends. The fashionable cafés along the street fill the air with the aroma of freshly made coffee, beckoning customers to take a seat.

The ambience takes on a lovely shift as Chapel Street stretches into Prahran. An attraction that draws both residents and tourists is the lively Prahran Market, where they may browse fresh fruit, handcrafted items, and unusual treasures. With the vivid hues of fruits and vegetables contrasting with the fragrant scents of freshly baked bread and unusual spices, the market is a sensory feast.

Windsor's bohemian flair becomes apparent as one travels farther along Chapel Street. The area is transformed into an outdoor gallery that honors creativity and self-expression thanks to the street art that covers the walls. Adorable boutiques and vintage shops entice with their abundance of gently used clothing and unique trinkets.

Chapel Street is a culinary adventure that entices the senses; it's more than simply a place to buy. The Boulevard is lined with a variety of restaurants, ranging from posh restaurants to intimate brunch cafes, all of which add to Melbourne's status as a foodie paradise. Dining al fresco at sidewalk tables fosters a social atmosphere that extends onto the street as patrons enjoy their meals there.

Chapel Street comes to life as the day fades into the evening. Bars and taverns teeming with life, their façade aglow with neon lights, call out to those seeking a vibrant ambience. Live music wafts into the streets, providing a musical underscoring to the evening as revelers take in the city's thriving nightlife.

Chapel Street reflects Melbourne's multifaceted personality and is more than just a roadway. It's a dynamic tale that changes with every stride. Chapel Street welcomes you to immerse yourself in the diverse range of experiences that constitute this renowned Melbourne destination, regardless of your interests in fashion, cuisine, or art.

Melbourne Central Retail Centre

Located in the center of the city, Melbourne Central Shopping is a retail oasis that goes beyond the typical shopping experience. You're engulfed in an immersive setting that suits every taste and desire as soon as you enter the expansive atrium, where modern architecture blends with a wide variety of retailers.

The landmark Shot Tower, with its historical importance set against the modernism of the commercial complex, is a testimony to Melbourne's industrial legacy. A broad panorama of the busy floors below, each showcasing a microcosm of lifestyle, fashion, and technological options, greets you as you mount the escalators.

Every consumer in Melbourne Central, from the trendsetter to the tech enthusiast, will be able to discover their niche thanks to the wide variety of brands and boutiques available. Premium clothing stores provide the newest designs, while tech centers provide the latest devices and accessories for those who like technology. Independent, quirky boutiques provide a touch of individuality with their carefully chosen merchandise, catering to those looking for one-of-a-kind items.

The environment is a synthesis of sensory experiences rather than simply being about business. Freshly brewed coffee fills the air as it comes from all of the cafés and restaurants that are scattered around the mall. Both locals and visitors relax in these areas, recharging between shopping excursions as their chats merge with the bustle of activities.

The distinctive glass dome of Melbourne Central's architecture allows natural light to spill over the store floors, fostering a warm atmosphere. The dynamic aspect created by the play of light and shadow enhances the space's visual appeal and establishes it as a destination for both commerce and architectural appreciation.

The intricate design promotes exploration since there are secret passageways and crevices just waiting to be found. The shopping experience is given a creative boost by art installations and interactive exhibits, which transform Melbourne Central into a vibrant cultural hub that goes beyond the conventional retail model.

Melbourne Central changes as the day gives way to night. A mesmerizing nighttime atmosphere is produced by the flashing lights of the stores and the radiance of the famous clock tower. The city's nightlife and the retail district coexist together, with pubs and restaurants welcoming customers seeking a post-shopping social or gastronomic treat.

Melbourne Central Shopping is more than simply a place to shop; it's an experience in the city, a voyage through a carefully designed environment that captures Melbourne's energy. It's a location where business, culture, and community come together, enticing people to engage in experiences that capture the lively essence of this global metropolis rather than merely buy.

Chapter 8

Parks and Gardens in Melbourne

Royal Botanic Gardens in Melbourne

Situated in the center of the city, the Melbourne Royal Botanic Gardens are a green paradise that captivates tourists with its lush landscapes and floral marvels. This famous 94-acre garden is a living mosaic of biodiversity rather than just a collection of plants.

The sound of rustling leaves and the scent of blossoming flowers fill the air as you pass through the elaborate gates, resulting in a sensory experience that is very captivating. The carefully designed gardens have a wide variety of plant species, ranging from native Australian flora to exotic examples from across the world. As you go along the winding paths, you come upon a floral display that goes beyond simple gardening.

The focal point of the gardens, the Ornamental Lake, reflects the surrounding foliage and offers a serene setting for the colorful flora exhibits. The lake, which is bordered by graceful swans and lined with willows, has a calm, peaceful beauty that begs for reflection and leisurely strolls.

Layers of historical value are added to the gardens by integrating them with their natural beauty. One fascinating terraced garden that demonstrates the Victorian era's obsession with geological structures is Guilfoyle's Volcano. It is a living relic that invites people to study its distinctive design and discover the background history that influenced it.

An immersive experience through a reconstructed eucalyptus forest is provided by the Australian Forest Walk for individuals looking for a closer connection with the natural world. The tall trees, aromatic air, and sporadic calls of local avian species whisk guests away to the core of Australia's natural environment.

Events and educational activities enhance the experience even further by introducing guests of all ages to the marvels of plant life. The Melbourne Royal Botanic Gardens provide programs for both the inquisitive beginner and the experienced botanist, including guided tours and seasonal exhibits.

Apart from housing valuable flora, the gardens function as a center of cultural activities. The Ian Potter Foundation Children's Garden offers young explorers an engaging environment that helps them develop a love of nature at a young age. The Garden Shop and Terrace Café provide guests with the chance to deepen their experience by offering botanical mementos and a spot to relax in the breathtaking surroundings.

The gardens' characteristics shift with the seasons, providing an ever-changing display of hues and textures. Every visit reveals a new chapter in the continuous tale of this horticultural masterpiece, from the vivid colors of spring blooms to the golden palette of fall leaves.

The Melbourne Royal Botanic Gardens, to put it simply, go beyond what is often associated with a botanical garden. They are a living artwork that honors the natural world's beauty, promotes environmental consciousness, and offers a haven for leisure and contemplation in the middle of one of Australia's fastest-growing towns.

Melbourne's Yarra Park

Yarra Park is a vibrant urban paradise that seamlessly integrates sports, leisure, and a hint of tranquility in the middle of Melbourne. It is located next to the well-known Melbourne Cricket Ground (MCG).

The lively spirit of Melbourne's athletic culture envelops you as soon as you enter Yarra Park. Huge and imposing, the MCG is an architectural wonder that dominates the skyline and provides a spectacular backdrop for AFL showdowns and exciting cricket matches. Whether they have tickets to the game or are just there to experience the infectious enthusiasm, passionate spectators swarm the park, which transforms into an expanded stadium for important events.

When the bustle of tourists subsides, Yarra Park becomes a sanctuary for leisure and outdoor pursuits. Families, exercise enthusiasts, and picnickers are all welcome on the expansive grounds. Here, the sound of youngsters playing and the rhythmic thud of footballs being kicked about combine to create a symphony of leisure set against the background of the city skyline.

Alongside the park, the Yarra River flows gently, providing beautiful scenery and a peaceful haven from the bustle of the city. Taking a trip along the riverfront offers a revitalizing viewpoint, with the park's lushness on one side and the city on the other. The lively mood in the park during athletic events is a far cry from the peace of the riverfront.

The variety of Yarra Park's vegetation gives the cityscape a hint of organic beauty. During hot days, pockets of cool relief are created by towering trees that provide shade. When flowerbeds bloom, they bring vibrant hues that go well with the seasons' constant change. It is a location where the vitality of the city and the natural world live together.

Yarra Park is a place where people come together to create a sense of community, not just a place to visit. Weekend picnics are enjoyed by families, friends play pickup games of sports, and runners navigate the park's maze-like network of paths. The conviviality and feeling of shared pleasure weave a distinctive social fabric that characterizes the park.

Apart from providing recreational facilities, Yarra Park also acts as a venue for cultural events and public gatherings. The park is transformed into a venue for a variety of events that appeal to the wide range of interests of Melbourne's citizens and tourists, including outdoor concerts and community festivals.

Yarra Park's diverse appeal entices visitors seeking the thrill of athletic events, the peace of a riverbank stroll, or the happiness of an informal picnic. It is a reflection of Melbourne's vibrant character, where the calm of the natural world blends with the fast-paced metropolitan life to create an environment that is in tune with the city's pulse.

Fitzroy Gardens, Melbourne

The Fitzroy Gardens are a timeless haven tucked away in the center of Melbourne that seamlessly blends horticulture, history, and a peaceful diversion from the hustle and bustle of the city. This 26-hectare carefully designed oasis is more than just a collection of green areas; it's a living reminder of the city's rich history as well as a refuge for those looking to unwind in the embrace of nature.

You feel at ease as soon as you step onto the grounds. Centuries-old trees, such as majestic English elms and local eucalypts, provide a towering canopy that forms a green cathedral that inspires reflection. The delicate scent of blooms permeates the air, and the symphony of songbirds enhances the whole sensory experience with a musical dimension.

The historic Conservatory, a Victorian-era masterpiece that presents colorful flower displays all year long, is one of Fitzroy Gardens' most distinctive attractions. This architectural treasure takes guests to a bygone period when the beauty of horticulture meets the accuracy of classic architecture, thanks to its exquisite glass panels and complex ironwork.

Nestled in the grounds, the magnificent Captain Cook's Cottage serves as an additional point of connection between guests and Melbourne's history. Originally brought from England, this painstakingly restored home provides a physical connection to the city's colonial past. A peek into the life of one of history's most famous explorers may be had by meandering around its charming chambers and investigating the little garden that surrounds it.

A whimsical touch is added by the miniature Tudor village located inside the grounds, which perfectly captures the spirit of Olde England with its thatched-roof homes and quaint gardens. It's a charming surprise that invites guests to stroll along its cobblestone walkways and savor the charming charm of a bygone period.

Fitzroy Gardens is a dynamic place that changes with the seasons rather than a static tableau. In spring, the elaborate designs of the flowerbeds explode with color, while in summer, the cool, shaded walkways provide a welcome respite from the heat. Autumn uses a palette of reds and golds to paint the gardens, while winter displays a new type of beauty when the trees' graceful structure is revealed by their naked branches.

Young and old alike are enthralled by the fairy tree, which is covered with elaborate carvings that portray fantastical settings and figures. It's a living work of art that gives the gardens a magical touch while serving as a reminder to guests that anything is possible in this urban haven where the commonplace may become spectacular.

The beautifully designed ponds and winding trails provide a peaceful haven for individuals in search of peace. The peaceful environment that promotes meditation is enhanced by the sound of falling leaves, the reflection of weeping willows in quiet ponds, and the sporadic sighting of local ducks.

Fitzroy Gardens is more than just a place to visit; it's a mosaic of experiences designed to suit the wide range of interests and preferences of its guests. The gardens provide a mosaic of Melbourne's past, present, and ever-expanding promise of its future, catering to the interests of history buffs, nature lovers, and anybody else looking for a peaceful place to ponder.

Chapter 9

Melbourne Sports and Recreation

Cricket Grounds in Melbourne (MCG)

In the sports industry, the Melbourne Cricket Ground (MCG), sometimes known as "The G," is a well-known landmark. Located in the center of Melbourne, Australia, this enormous stadium symbolizes a wealth of athletic events, customs, and history that goes beyond its tangible dimensions.

Built as a simple cricket pitch in 1853, the MCG has developed into a major international sports arena. Its vast grounds have seen many cricket matches and important occasions, including the first-ever Test match in 1877. The MCG is revered by cricket enthusiasts as a sacred field where luminaries like Shane Warne and Sir Donald Bradman carved their names into the history of the game.

But the MCG isn't only for cricket; it's welcomed a wide range of sports as well, turning into a flexible location for rugby, Australian Rules football, and even concerts. During the summer, cricket fanatics fill the sacred grass, but in the winter, it becomes a football fan's battlefield, creating an environment of unyielding passion and commitment.

Beyond its importance to sports, the MCG is a magnificent architectural structure. Steeped in history, the majestic stands serve as mute witnesses to the tides of time. Huge and towering, the Great Southern Stand provides fans with a clear perspective of the athletic spectacle taking place on the field. An outstanding example of the mutually beneficial link between sport and urban life is the Melbourne Cricket Ground silhouette set against the backdrop of the city.

The MCG's atmosphere reaches well beyond its field of play. Within its grounds is the National Sports Museum, which allows tourists to explore the athletic history of the country while preserving the legacy of Australian sporting accomplishments. A pilgrimage for sports fans, the MCG Tour provides a close-up look inside the inner sanctuary of the stadium, revealing untold tales and behind-the-scenes views that deepen the visitor's bond with this hallowed venue.

The MCG has had difficulties recently adjusting to the dynamic nature of international sports and the influence of other factors. However, its tenacity and unwavering spirit are a reflection of the athletes who have walked its field throughout the years.

The Melbourne Cricket Ground is essentially more than simply a stadium—rather, it is a real, breathing example of how sport can bring people together, cross borders, and leave a lasting legacy. One can't help but feel a feeling of awe for this historic institution that has lasted the test of time and continues to be a beacon for sports aficionados worldwide as the sun sets over the MCG, throwing its golden light on the hallowed ground.

Melbourne Park hosts the Australian Open

Every year, Melbourne Park hosts the Australian Open, a tennis spectacle that celebrates athleticism, ability, and unshakable enthusiasm beyond the realm of sports. This legendary event, one of the four Grand Slam competitions, has come to be associated with exciting matches, heartfelt wins, and a joyous vibe that permeates Melbourne.

In January, Melbourne Park, which is tucked away in the center of the energetic metropolis, becomes a tennis haven. Under the Australian heat, the immaculate blue courts provided the backdrop for fierce fights and unforgettable memories. As tennis players from all over the world congregate at this athletic haven, cultures collide and infectious energy permeates the atmosphere.

The allure of the Australian Open is found in both the exceptional tennis matches and the distinctive Melbourne atmosphere it provides. The date of the event in Australia's summertime provides the ideal balance of outdoor entertainment and professional tennis. While savoring delicious treats from the lively food courts and basking in the sun, spectators may also enjoy live music and entertainment that adds to the celebratory atmosphere.

The main arena at Melbourne Park, the Rod Laver Arena, is the place to go for the biggest matches. This stadium, which bears the name of the renowned

Australian tennis player, has seen the ascent of champions and the writing of tennis history. The heated confrontations taking place on the court are set against an unmatched background created by the electrifying atmosphere inside the stadium, which is propelled by the impassioned cheers of the spectators.

Outside of the main arena, spectators may have exciting close-up interactions with their favorite players on the outer courts, which also hold exciting events. Tennis greats develop their abilities on the practice courts, which provide an intimate look at the commitment and planning needed to compete at the highest level.

The Australian Open is a cultural phenomenon that unites people rather than merely being a competitive event. The Grand Slam Oval encourages a feeling of community among tennis enthusiasts with its bustling fan zones and engaging exhibitions. Everyone feels like they're a part of something very great during the event, regardless of whether they're a seasoned fan or just a casual spectator.

The fact that the world's top tennis players come to the event adds to its relevance on a worldwide scale.

The matches involving the best tennis players in the world, such as Roger Federer, Rafael Nadal, Novak Djokovic, Serena Williams, and up-and-coming talents, create unforgettable memories for the spectators.

As the Australian Open comes to a close and the sun sets over Melbourne Park, an everlasting legacy of sports prowess, friendship, and the unbreakable spirit of competitiveness is left behind. For both sports fans and casual spectators, it's not simply a tennis tournament; it's a spectacle that captures the spirit of Melbourne's dynamic culture and the attractiveness of the game worldwide.

Yarra River cycling

Riding a bicycle along Melbourne's Yarra River is an immersive experience that combines the bright vitality of the city with the tranquility of nature. Cyclists looking for a distinctive and revitalizing experience will find a magnificent background as the Yarra River meanders through the center of the city.

Riding a bike along the Yarra River reveals a diverse range of scenery. With their abundance of flora, the riverbanks provide a peaceful haven from the bustle of the city. Every pedal stroke is accompanied by the calming sound of flowing water, producing a melodic symphony that fits the ride's pace.

There is something for every kind of cyclist, from casual riders to serious aficionados, on the Yarra River trail. The bike paths are kept up well and provide a smooth path for exploration as they meander beside the river. Cyclists are exposed to a kaleidoscope of sights as they ride; from famous metropolitan skylines to obscure areas of unspoiled beauty, every curve in the route unveils a new side of Melbourne's allure.

Seeing the wide variety of plants and animals that live along the riverbanks is one of the best parts of riding the Yarra River. Birdwatchers and nature lovers may find refuge in the parks and reserves that border the bike routes. Cycling is made more enjoyable by the stunning view of colorful parrots darting between trees, gorgeous pelicans floating on the lake, and the odd kookaburra laughing.

An additional approach to accessing some of Melbourne's cultural treasures is along the Yarra River. The route takes on a new cultural dimension as you pedal by iconic locations like Federation Square, the Royal Botanic Gardens, and the Arts Centre Melbourne. Melbourne's distinct beauty is embodied in the way that nature, culture, and urban life are all seamlessly integrated along the riverbanks.

The lively ambiance of Southbank, where the Yarra River flows gently and the city skyline makes for a breathtaking background, often draws cyclists. Bike enthusiasts are welcome to take a leisurely stop in this lively sector, which is dotted with cafés, restaurants, and entertainment venues. While enjoying a tasty meal or a cup of coffee, riders may take in the picturesque surroundings.

The Yarra River opens up as a conduit for discovery as the cycling adventure progresses, beckoning cyclists to find undiscovered treasures along its banks. A feeling of suspense and expectation is created around every curve of the river by the picturesque neighborhoods, riverside sculptures, and attractive bridges that contribute to the whole experience.

The Yarra River is transformed into a beautiful painting in the golden light of dusk, reflecting city lights on its serene waters. Riding along its banks at this enchanted hour is a sensory extravaganza, with the soft colors of twilight enhancing the natural beauty of the surroundings and providing each rider with an immersive and unforgettable experience.

Riding a bicycle down the Yarra River is essentially a trip that unites Melbourne's natural, cultural, and urban aspects rather than just being a physical exercise. Whether cycling for health, a social ride with companions, or a solitary tour of the city's best-kept secrets, the Yarra River offers a blank canvas on which riders may create an unforgettable and fulfilling experience.

Chapter 10

Melbourne Entertainment and Nightlife

Theatres in Melbourne and Live Entertainment

Melbourne has a thriving and active cultural environment, especially in terms of live events and theaters. The city's theatrical scene offers a wide range of choices for both ardent theatergoers and casual viewers, weaving together a complex tapestry of invention, history, and variety.

The Melbourne Theatre Company, a mainstay of the city's performing arts scene, is one such facility. The company, which is well-known for its captivating performances, presents a wide variety of plays, from modern pieces to classic tragedies, always pushing the limits of theatrical expression and narrative.

For those in search of a more innovative experience, the Arts Centre Melbourne is a creative lighthouse. There are many theaters in this cultural complex, and they all feature different acts, such as opera, dance, and experimental theater. Not only is the distinctive spire of the Arts Centre a visual icon, but it also represents Melbourne's dedication to the arts.

The Princess Theatre, a heritage-listed space, gives the city's theatrical offerings a hint of the past. The Princess Theatre, with its elaborate design and rich history, has grown to be a popular venue for big-budget theatrical plays and successful musicals.

Melbourne's performing arts sector benefits from its laneways, which are well-known for their street art and hidden treasures. Small, alternative venues like The Butterfly Club provide up-and-coming performers and experimental shows on stage, encouraging a grassroots, neighborhood-based approach to theater.

Comedians from all over the globe travel to Melbourne each year to demonstrate their skills at the Melbourne International Comedy Festival, which brings comedy to the city's cultural scene. There is something for every humorous taste on the festival's varied roster, which fosters a spirit of humor and friendship throughout the city.

Melbourne welcomes outdoor events and public art pieces in addition to conventional theaters. Occasions such as the Melbourne Fringe Festival encourage artists to push boundaries and interact in novel ways with audiences, celebrating the unusual.

Melbourne's live performances and theaters, in short, provide a vibrant fusion of innovation and heritage, guaranteeing that the city will always be a center of creativity. For those who are enthralled by the allure of live performances, Melbourne's theatrical offerings provide a varied and stimulating experience, regardless of whether they are attracted to the intimacy of hidden treasures or the grandeur of major venues.

Melbourne's Nightclubs and Bars

For those looking for amusement when the sun goes down, Melbourne's nightlife offers a kaleidoscope of experiences woven with the colorful threads of pubs and nightclubs. For those who want to party late into the night, the city has a wide range of possibilities, from stylish rooftop pubs to energetic dance floors.

Melbourne's laneways are popular for their varied attractiveness during the day, but at night they become vibrant centers of nightlife. The city's drinking culture is given an aura of mystery and exclusivity by hidden pubs that are nestled behind modest facades. These underground bars often include talented mixologists who create visually arresting and flavor-bursting concoctions.

Melbourne fits the bill for individuals who like to sip their cocktails while taking in a glimpse of the sky. Rooftop bars with expansive views of the metropolitan skyline, such as Naked in the Sky and Siglo, offer the ideal setting for an indulgent and convivial evening. An air of sophistication and ease is created by the contrast between drinking drinks and seeing the city's lights twinkle.

Melbourne's pulse quickens with a varied choice of alternatives when it comes to nightclubs. Every musical preference is catered to on the city's dance floors, from hip-hop rhythms to electronic sounds. Famous locations like Onesixone and Revolver Upstairs are well known for their upbeat ambiance and immersive soundtracks, which lure people out to dance long into the morning.

Melbourne's Chapel Street is a popular destination for nightlife, with a variety of hip pubs and exciting clubs. With interactive features like a concealed ball pit, Pawn & Co., and other places showcasing the precinct's contagious enthusiasm, the celebrations extend beyond the music and refreshments.

The city's various venues that feature both local and international talent are proof of its dedication to live music. The Toff in Town and Cherry Bar are well-known for their cozy interiors that let fans of music interact closely with their idols.

Melbourne's nightlife is a vast mosaic that isn't limited to any one district, all of which add to the city's image as a playground for night owls. The refined atmosphere of a cocktail bar, the throbbing excitement of a nightclub, or the soul-stirring sounds of live music—whichever you prefer—Melbourne's pubs and nightclubs guarantee that the night is never too old or boring.

Events and festivals in Melbourne

Melbourne is a party city, and the wide range of festivals and events held there all year long captures the vibrant energy of the city's citizens. Melbourne's calendar is a tapestry woven with colorful events that entice both residents and tourists to join in the fun, from gastronomic pleasures to cultural extravaganzas.

The laughter that reverberates through the city streets is the start of the Melbourne International Comedy Festival. Comedians from all over the world pour into Melbourne, transforming the city into an unrestricted comedy playground. The event is a highlight for anybody looking for a lot of laughs because of its wide program, which guarantees that there is something to tickle every funny bone.

The landscape of festivals changes with the seasons. The Melbourne Food and Wine Festival showcases the city's culinary excellence and tantalizes the senses. This festival celebrates the variety and inventiveness of Melbourne's food sector by transforming the city into a gourmet utopia with events hosted by renowned chefs and secret alley feasts.

Melbourne is illuminated by White Night Melbourne, a stunning show of art and light. Famous sites are transformed into captivating projection screens for a single, amazing night, and the streets come alive with art installations and entertainment. It's an evening event that captivates people and turns the city into a surreal place.

The Melbourne International Arts Festival is a prominent event in the arts and culture sector, offering a varied schedule of shows, exhibits, and other activities. This festival highlights the city's dedication to encouraging innovation and pushing creative limits with its lineup of avant-garde theater and boundary-breaking visual arts.

Melbourne's passion for music is shown during occasions like Melbourne Music Week, when the diverse music landscape of the city takes center stage. The festival's peaceful atmosphere, created by a blend of local and international musicians, reverberates across both prominent venues and hidden gems.

The Melbourne Fashion Festival prioritizes runway elegance for fashion fans. This event turns the city into a sartorial showcase, where creativity and innovation in the fashion industry take center stage, including both known fashion companies and up-and-coming designers.

Sports fans swarm Melbourne for occasions such as the Australian Open, which ignites the city with the passion of a Grand Slam tennis match. A pinnacle of the horse racing season, the Melbourne Cup Carnival transforms Flemington Racecourse into a show of opulent costumes, exciting entertainment, and, of course, exciting racing.

Essentially, Melbourne's celebrations of community, innovation, and variety are reflected in its festivals and events, which are a monument to the city's lively character. Melbourne is a city that understands how to throw a celebration unlike any other since every event has its own distinct flavor and mood, which adds yet another layer to the rich tapestry that characterizes Melbourne's cultural identity.

Chapter 11

Day Trips from Melbourne

Great Ocean Road in Melbourne

Melbourne is the starting point for one of the most amazing picturesque drives in the world, the Great Ocean Road, which is tucked away along Australia's southeast coast. This famous road, which spans more than 240 kilometers, travels through a variety of landscapes and provides an enthralling fusion of natural beauty and cultural encounters.

Beginning in Melbourne, the city eventually gives way to breathtaking coastline views as you travel. The Great Ocean Road reveals rocky cliffs, immaculate beaches, and verdant rainforests as it unfurls like a beautiful tapestry. Every turn reveals a different aspect of Australia's stunning coastline, giving visitors an immersive experience.

The gem in the road's crown is the Twelve Apostles, a group of limestone stacks that rise magnificently from the Southern Ocean. With the setting sun as a background, these monoliths—sculpted by ages of wind and waves—create a bizarre scene. The way that light and shadow interact creates a dynamic picture that changes with the hour, providing nature lovers and photographers with a constantly changing backdrop on which to work.

Going further, the London Arch and Loch Ard Gorge beckon, each with its own story of natural development and marine drama. These sites encourage reflection on the passing of time and the tenacity of nature, in addition to showcasing the ocean's sheer force.

The Great Otway National Park reveals a beautiful tapestry of ancient rainforests beyond the marvels of the shore. Tall eucalyptus trees provide a canopy for a variety of plants and animals, making it a sanctuary for hikers and wildlife lovers alike. Moments of tranquility are provided by waterfalls that tumble through the verdant surroundings, among this verdant wildness.

Throughout the Great Ocean Road, you'll get the chance to experience the relaxed coastal lifestyle and sample local food in quaint seaside villages like Lorne and Apollo Bay. Enjoying delectable seafood or leisurely wandering along immaculate beaches, these tour stops provide the ideal combination of leisure and discovery.

Essentially, the Great Ocean Road is more than simply a road; it tells the story of Australia's breathtaking natural scenery, carved into the Victoria coast's cliffs and beaches. Things encourage visitors to take things slowly, take in the sea air, and be in awe of the beauties that nature and time have fashioned. This well-known pathway is proof of the alluring beauty that is waiting for those who are brave enough to follow its meandering course.

Wine Region of the Yarra Valley

Tucked away in the gentle rolling hills just outside of Melbourne's busy metropolitan area, the Yarra Valley Wine Region is a fascinating mosaic of vineyards, cellar doors, and culinary experiences. This area, which is well-known for both its exquisite wines and its stunning scenery, provides a sensory experience that goes beyond simple tasting and instead immerses one in the craft of winemaking and the abundance of nature.

The well-groomed rows of grapevines appear to dance to the soft rhythms of the air as you stroll through the Yarra Valley, enveloping the surrounding area in a serene aura. Numerous grape varieties find their optimal terroir in the region's cold environment and good soil. This is a very productive area for Chardonnay and Pinot Noir, and the wines that are produced have a specific flavor that is a consequence of the special mix of soil, climate, and skill of the vintner.

Not only are the many cellar doors scattered over the landscape locations for wine tastings, but they also serve as windows into the lives of passionate vintners. Every vineyard has a history—a story that is revealed with each bottle that is opened. The Yarra Valley is a refuge for oenophiles seeking variety in their tasting experiences, offering a mosaic of styles and ideologies from family-owned estates to avant-garde producers pushing the frontiers of winemaking.

Stop at renowned vineyards where the craft of sparkling wine is celebrated, such as Domaine Chandon. Every flute has a lively character that reflects the lively nature of the area. Smaller, boutique wineries, on the other hand, encourage you to find undiscovered treasures, where exclusive releases and cozy surroundings foster a sense of exploration and exclusivity.

The Yarra Valley is a culinary paradise where farm-to-table dining and vineyards often cohabit. It's not just about wine. Savor the bounty of the region, along with handcrafted cheeses, delicious foods, and wines that complement each other well. The culinary scene in the valley is an investigation of the harmony between the wealth of the area and the inventiveness of its chefs, a celebration of tastes.

The magnificent vistas and outdoor activities of the Yarra Valley extend beyond its wineries and dining experiences. A bird's-eye view of the vine-covered hills may be obtained via hot-air balloon trips, while trekking paths wind through verdant scenery to uncover undiscovered gems of the environment.

The rich notes of wine, the visual poetry of vineyards, and the gastronomic crescendo all come together to produce a memorable composition that is the Yarra Valley Wine Region. It is, in short, a sensory symphony. This area welcomes you to enjoy the present, recognize the artistry, and bask in the beautiful fusion of nature and human innovation, regardless of your level of experience with wine or your wanderlust.

Parks on Phillip Island

Situated in close proximity to Melbourne, Phillip Island Nature Parks entice visitors with a harmonic fusion of immaculate scenery, fascinating animals, and charming coastal ambience. Encircled by the azure seas of the Bass Strait, this picturesque retreat presents itself as a refuge for people who love the outdoors and want to get away from the bustle of the city.

The iconic Penguin Parade is without a doubt Phillip Island's main draw. The captivating sight of little penguins waddling ashore after a day of fishing lights up the coastline as the sun sets. The tourists, enthralled by the wonder of this natural phenomenon, congregate in expectation of this nightly parade, which is a tribute to nature's splendor.

The island's shoreline provides expansive views that extend to the horizon beyond the cute penguins. The windswept beaches, quiet coves, and craggy cliffs combine to provide a serene backdrop that begs reflection and a close relationship with the unadulterated beauty of the Southern Ocean. The Nobbies provide an unmatched viewpoint for seeing seals and seabirds in their native environment because of the boardwalks that are located on the brink of the cliff.

Go inland to see the verdant surroundings of the Churchill Island Heritage Farm. This operational farm, rich in history, provides an insight into the pastoral lifestyle of the first Australian settlers. Discover the historic gardens, see demonstrations of sheep shearing, and stroll about the farmland, where the rustic charm and well-maintained homesteads bring the past to life.

The Koala Conservation Centre offers a rare chance for anyone who has a soft spot for birds to see these famous marsupials in their natural eucalyptus environment. Koalas are contentedly tucked up in the limbs of trees as you stroll along treetop boardwalks, which is evidence of Phillip Island's dedication to protecting wildlife.

The Phillip Island Grand Prix Circuit, a sanctuary for fans of racing, is another example of how Phillip Island Nature Parks embraces the sky. This iconic track, home of the Australian Motorcycle Grand Prix, offers visitors the chance to experience the exhilaration of fast racing or to enjoy a leisurely lap and take in the exhilarating atmosphere.

The attraction of the island is not limited to its charming villages, where artisanal shops, seafood restaurants, and local markets weave a tapestry of real experiences. Savor locally produced wines, indulge in freshly caught seafood, and experience Phillip Island's relaxed seaside lifestyle.

The Phillip Island Nature Parks are essentially a miniature version of Australia's varied topography and amazing biodiversity. This refuge allows you to step away from the everyday and re-connect with the exceptional aspects of the natural world, whether you're attracted to the island's rich cultural tapestry, the captivating Penguin Parade, or both.

Chapter 12

Practical Tips for Travelers

Climate and the Ideal Time to Go to Melbourne

Melbourne, Australia, has dynamic weather patterns that are well-known and may be linked to its geographic position. Melbourne, which is located in the southeast of the nation, has a moderate climate with distinct seasons. It's essential to know the subtleties of Melbourne's weather in order to organize the best possible trip.

September to November is a great time to visit Melbourne in the spring. This time of year brings with it a lovely and energizing vibe as the city is decked out in flowering flowers and the temperatures gradually climb. Melbourne's floral splendor in spring is shown at the renowned Melbourne International Flower and Garden Show, which is held in March every year.

Warmer weather throughout the summer, which runs from December to February, makes it the perfect season for festivals and outdoor activities. Events like the Australian Open, which draw sports fans and tennis fanatics from all over the world, bring the city to life. But, since summertime might bring very high temperatures, be ready for sporadic heatwaves.

Fall, which lasts from March to May, offers a temperate environment with chilly nights. The colorful metamorphosis of the leaves, which produces magnificent vistas, is what defines this season. Wandering around Melbourne's parks, including the Royal Botanic Gardens, during this time of year offers a peaceful experience among the shifting foliage.

June through August is when winter arrives, bringing with it lower temperatures and sporadic downpours. Even though Melbourne has mild winters compared to other regions of the globe, it's still important to dress in layers for comfort. In August, the city welcomes the Melbourne International Film Festival, which provides movie buffs with a cultural getaway.

The ideal time to visit Melbourne ultimately comes down to personal choice. While summer draws people looking for exciting outdoor events, spring and fall are often preferred for their pleasant weather and picturesque surroundings. Winter, on the other hand, offers a more sedate ambiance that is ideal for taking in the city's cultural activities and visiting indoor sights. Melbourne's dynamic and varied culture guarantees tourists an unforgettable experience all year round, regardless of the season.

Advice for Melbourne Public Transport

With a few insider tips, navigating Melbourne's public transport system may be a snap. The city is home to a well-established and functional transportation system that includes buses, trains, trams, and even ferries. Here are some helpful hints to get the most out of using Melbourne's public transport system, whether you're a resident or just visiting.

1. Magic Myki Cards:
Your pass to Melbourne's public transportation paradise is the Myki card. Get one from authorized

merchants, tram stops, and rail stations. Prior to boarding, remember to top up your card, and don't forget to turn it on and off to guarantee accurate fare computation. It's the secret to opening up the marvels of the city's transit system.

2. Manner in Trams:
Melbourne is well-known for its historic tram system. Make sure you board trams at the front or back doors and get off by the middle door. Remember to give people in need preferential seats. Trams are a great way to see the city and get a distinctive perspective of Melbourne's energetic streets.

3. Overview of Trains:
Melbourne's trains are a dependable option if you're going anywhere beyond the city center. Linking many rail lines together, Flinders Street Station is a significant hub. If you're in a hurry, check the schedule for the next departure and keep an eye out for fast trains.

4. Journeys on Buses:
Buses provide flexibility by traveling to places where trains and trams cannot. Utilizing internet resources or smartphone applications, familiarize

yourself with bus routes and stops. Buses are a fantastic way to see Melbourne's many areas.

5. Night Network Wisdom: After dark, Melbourne's Night Network keeps the city linked. Key routes are serviced by night trams and buses, which provide a quick and safe means of transportation at night. Recall that the Myki card is with you on your nighttime adventures as well.

6. Bike & Ride: Melbourne promotes an environmentally conscious and healthy way of living. Cycling and public transportation may be combined thanks to the bike storage options available at many train stations. By using an integrated approach, you may discover the city's natural and urban attractions.

7. Tracking in Real Time:
Use real-time tracking applications to be informed. These applications let you precisely plan your trip by giving you real-time information on the arrivals and departures of public transportation. They are quite helpful in preventing pointless wait periods.

8. Take a Look Around the Free Tram Zone:
With the Free Tram Zone in the center of

Melbourne, you may board and get off trams without tapping your Myki card. It's a great way to see the main sights without having to worry about paying for tickets.

All in all, Melbourne's public transit is a masterfully coordinated symphony of buses, trains, and trams. Accept the Myki card, get familiar with the ins and outs of each form of transportation, and you'll soon be gliding around this dynamic metropolis' lively streets with ease.

Local customs and etiquette in Melbourne

Understanding and respecting the local manners and traditions will greatly improve your experience as you enter Melbourne's vibrant cultural tapestry. Given that Melburnians are renowned for their friendliness and diversity, navigating the social scene with a little bit of insider knowledge can make your stay in the city more pleasurable.

1. Reverence for Coffee Culture:
In Melbourne, where there is a well-known coffee culture, asking for a "long black" or "flat white" is almost a given. Cafés are meeting places for people,

and you should usually stay and enjoy the talk while sipping your coffee. Although it's not required, leaving a tip at a café is appreciated when you get excellent service.

2. Courtesy in Public Transportation:

Being courteous is essential while utilizing public transportation, particularly trams. To prevent delays, provide room for people to exit before boarding, volunteer your seat to those in need, and have your Myki card available. It's a group dance that guarantees a courteous and easy trip.

3. Case Study:

In general, Australians love standing in lines. Line-waiting is an essential part of local etiquette, whether you're waiting for public transportation, placing an order, or getting into an event. Being patient is a shared social activity as well as a virtue.

4. Diversity Respect:

Melbourne's ethnic fabric is one of its greatest assets, and the city's culture is deeply rooted in tolerance for difference. Accept the diversity of languages, foods, and cultures that you will come across. It is quite welcome to participate in discussions with an open mind and sincere interest.

5. Active Interest in Sports:

Sports are very important to Melburnians, especially Australian Rules Football (AFL), cricket, and tennis. Talking about sports with locals is a great way to establish a connection. During a game, wearing the colors of your preferred team might start a conversation.

6. Appreciation of Art:

Melbourne is a creative hotspot, full of galleries, performing venues, and street art. Respecting and appreciating the street art movement is usual since it is seen as a form of public expression. A trip down one of the city's many alleys, such as Hosier Lane, offers a close-up view of this vibrant facet of the culture.

7. Relaxed Approach:

Although Melburnians work hard, the city has a carefree and easygoing vibe about it. Accept this leisurely pace, whether you're strolling about the many districts or enjoying a cup of coffee at a laneway café.

8. Conservation Awareness:

Melbourne is proud of its dedication to environmental sustainability. Recycling is ingrained in the locals' consciousness of the environment. To fit in with the local way of thinking, dispose of rubbish properly and take part in the city's eco-friendly programs.

9. Capri Fit Outfit:

The city of Melbourne is well known for having "four seasons in a day." Part of the knowledge of the locals is knowing how to prepare for unexpected weather changes. Wearing layers of clothing and carrying an umbrella can help you easily handle the city's constantly shifting weather.

Essentially, experiencing Melbourne's local etiquette is a combination of appreciating the city's distinctive features, honoring social standards, and accepting cultural diversity. Add a pinch of politeness and an open mind to the way people live here, and you'll find yourself irreversibly woven into Melbourne's vivid cultural tapestry.